When They Leave, We Stay Strong!

Written by

Elena Loredana Greenberg

Copyright © 2018 Elena Loredana Greenberg

All rights reserved.

ISBN: 978-1-7328247-0-6
ISBN-13: 978-1-7328247-0-6

Illustrated by Eugenia Reznik and Military Children

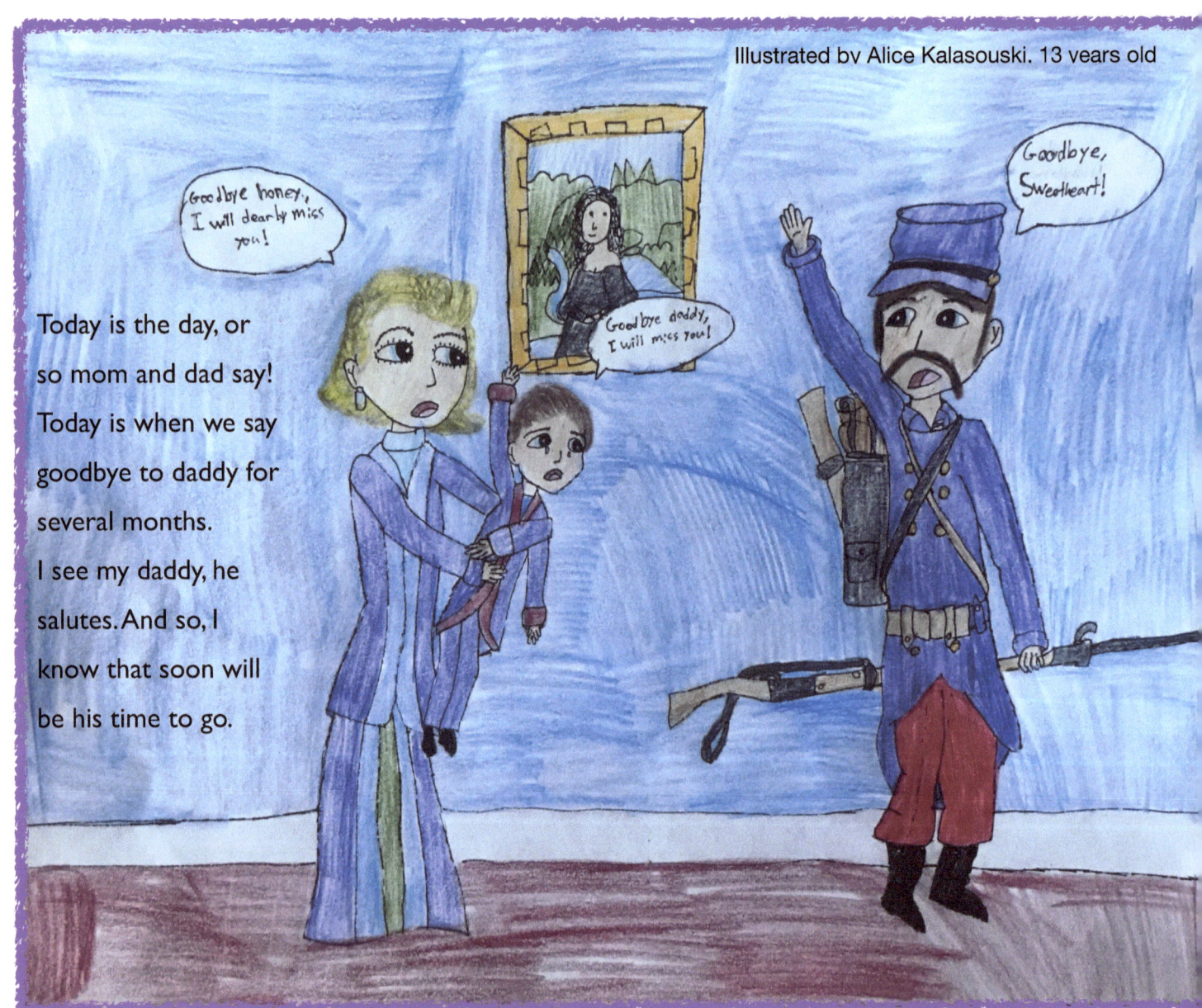

I look outside, and I see the plane. I get sad, and it is ok to feel that way. My dad is leaving, will be just mom and I for months to come.

I look around, I see familiar faces.
My daddy will have his friends with him, to help him do the things, that I get help from my friends too.

Illustrated by Daniel Tulloch, 11 years old

Dad gives me kisses and hugs us tight. He whispers to mommy`s ear " Honey it`s time to go, will miss you dearly both of you!" We wave goodbye, and we blow kisses as our dear hero goes further, following the path to the plane.

Illustrated by London Wheeler, 8 years old

I see Samantha, with her mom. They say hello and look so sad. As mommy sheds a tear says "When they leave, we stay strong. Let`s get the girls together soon". All will be alright; mommy whispers as we are walking to the car.

Illustrated by Ariyana Morey, 7 years old

Illustrated by Emma Dalton, 11 years old

While driving home, my mommy says that daddy will not call for the first week or so. He will travel and settle in, at the new place that will be his home.
And we make plans for weeks to come as those will be the hardest ones.

Illustrated by Xavier Matthew McKenna, 10 years old

I ask about my daddy because I want to know. If I will see him soon, and how will that go. And mommy tells me all, as she knows that this will help me grow.
She also says we need a daddy game to keep a little track on time.

Syria — Colorado

Daddy's time

our time

At home, we have a wall for daddy. We'll have a big watch that will show when the time will come for dad to sleep, to eat, and work. This is how we'll know when will be the time for him to call.

Illustrated by Ariyana Morey, 7 years old

Illustrated by Adrian Tita, 12 years old

We will go to the zoo and will find so many fun activities to do. We'll visit my friends and will make new ones too.
Mommy will make sure that every day will be the best.

Illustrated by Roxana Tita, 8 years old

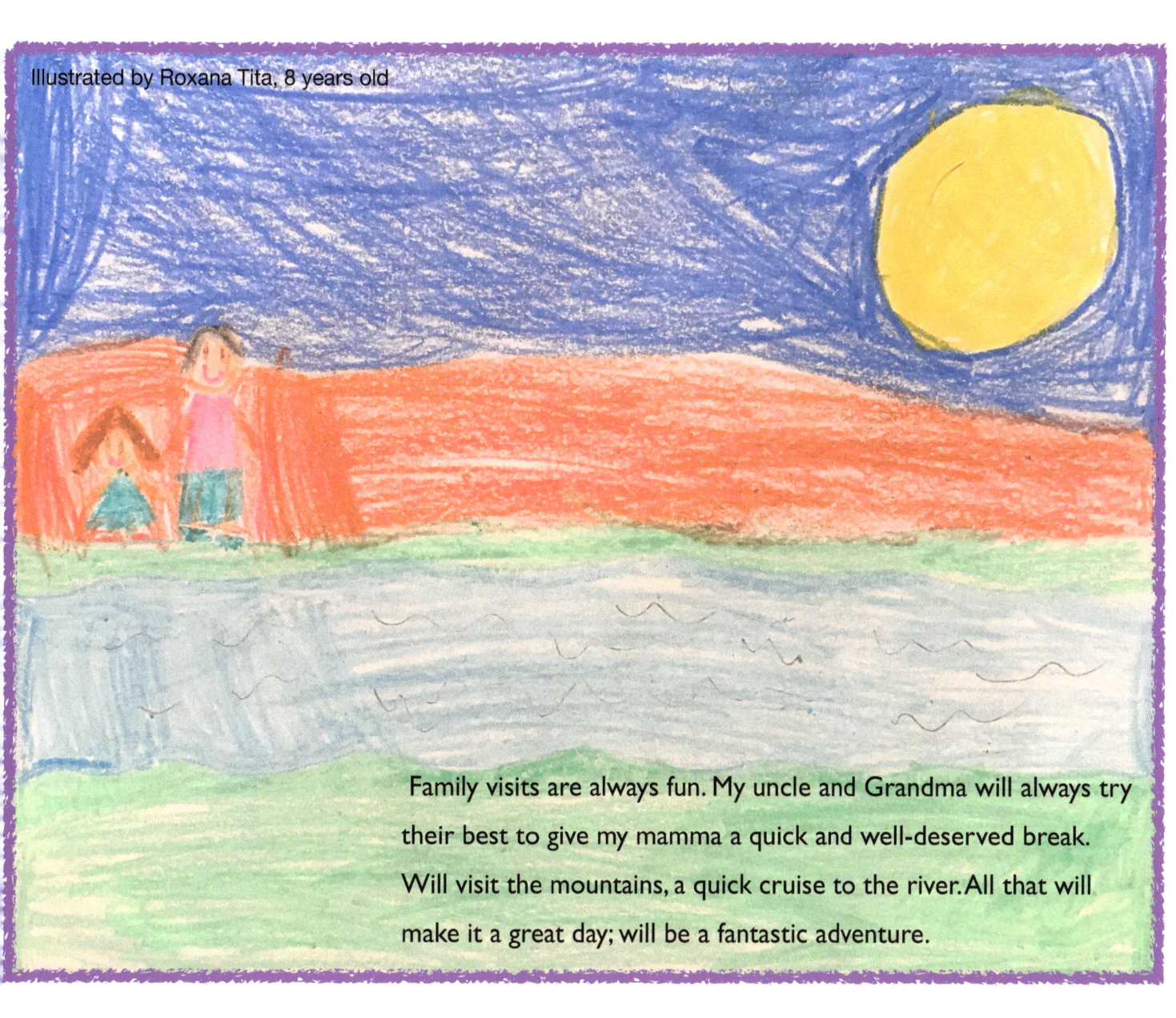

Family visits are always fun. My uncle and Grandma will always try their best to give my mamma a quick and well-deserved break. Will visit the mountains, a quick cruise to the river. All that will make it a great day; will be a fantastic adventure.

Illustrated by Alice Kalasouski, 13 years old

My mommy is funny. She says "don't worry honey", when I say that my doggy is sad. Together we go at the vet. We make sure that Walker is all set, to play and to chase. To run around and jump on the fence.

Illustrated by Gunnar Hirsch, 11 years old

In bed, I go as soon as sleepy time is here. I get so many kisses from my mommy, and since my daddy is not here, he sends me kisses in the sky.

Illustrated by Sarah Maria Greenberg, 4 years old

Today it will be fun. We wake up, and as soon as with breakfast we`re done, we'll go see my friends. At the daycare will be until dinner is almost ready.

Illustrated by Ashlyn Rae McKenna, 4 years old

With grandma we will play, or will go to her house to visit.
At least two or three times, until dad will come back to see us.

Illustrated by Emma Dalton, 11 years old

We'll plan some fun activities. Maybe we can go to Disney and a few trips to the Zoo.
Playdates with friends and walks to the park will make the time fly by.

Illustrated by Brooklyn Baca, 7 years old

Together with mom, will have a great time.
We will make new friends and play with
the old ones too.
If it is spring or a hot summer, we will pick
up flowers and watch the sunshine.

Illustrated by Sarah Maria Greenberg, 4 years old

We will dress warmly in the fall or winter and will go on a show. We can go for a hike or make a tiny snowman. No matter the season, patiently waiting for daddy it is our mission.

Illustrated by Mason Brazel, 9 years old

Illustrated by Cadence Hirsch, 10 years old

The winter is our favorite season. The blue sky and the magic I see when the snow falls over the trees. This year for Santa I have only one wish, my biggest desire is for dad to return. Under the Christmas tree or at the door, it will not matter as long as he will come home.

Illustrated by Dylan Brazel, 5 years old

The life won't stop, it will go on. But we will try to slow it down a little bit. So dad when comes, will play catch up in not much time.

When sad I get, and I might cry. My mommy holds me tight and whispers with all her might "when they leave; we stay strong!".
I may not see my dad in months, but sure I know that he loves us so!

Illustrated by Carter Wheeler, 7 years old

Illustrated by Alexander Miguel Madrid, 7 years

Today is the day when dad comes from far away.
As we reunite, we will focus on the family bond.

www.ingramcontent.com/pod-product-compliance
Lightning Source LLC
Chambersburg PA
CBHW041232040426
42444CB00002B/131